Ruth

Reme[mber]... [wh]er[ever]

fall ... [th]e[i]r

see the w[orld]

lies." Happiness & love

Becky

2-21-75

Fromm can teach about
The Art of Loving,

Lowen can preach about
Love and Orgasm,

and I can only write about
that which *I* know:

Surviving
The Loss of A Love.

Surviving
the Loss of a Love

and

the Survival Handbook

Surviving
the Loss of a Love

A Versemonger Press Book
Distributed to the trade by
Doubleday Inc.
Garden City, New York

morning.
we wake & snuggle.

after noon.
a phone call, california beckons.

evening.
the air port. a brutal good(?)bye.

night.
o my god. o my god.   o my god.

mourning.
again.

thursday: drowning in love.

friday: drowning in doubt.

saturday: drowning.

sunday: God, I can't drag my
self to church this morning
please make a house call.

it will never be the same.
I will never be the same.

you   came.
we   loved.
you   left.

I will survive   until I survive.

and one day I will
turn around and find
myself alive again.

and another day
another's path will
run parallel to mine
for a while.

and one another day
you will return
and I will see

It is not the same.

Life has many secrets.

Where you are tonight
is one of them.

Another, why, really,
did you go.

The world holds many wonders.

You are one of them.

will you return my call

or not
?

The Longest Night begins.

you cannot come into
my life
again.

don't try to enter
my mind with
your eyes.

it won't work.

I am inpenetrable.
aloof.
friendly, but distant.
kind, but cold.

this time
        you haven't a chance.

still,
your ten minute visit
will cause me
ten days
of pain.

how hard the forgetting.
how easy the remembering.

how cruel the process
that possesses me.

the ancient chinese had a
torture in which water was
dripped onto a person's face

        drop
         by
        drop

I know this torture well.

The Torture Of The Thousand Tears.

you came
and made
my house
our home

you left
making
our home
my asylum

I guess you had to no.
I guess I had to know.

I guess you had to go.
I guess I have to grow.

I remember thinking once
that it would be good
if you left because
then I could get some
Important Things
done.

since you've left I've done
nothing. nothing
is as important
as you.

it is as though you were
dead.

there is nothing to be
done.

only accept it . . .

and hurt.

I was
overcome,
and now
undone.

this september
will be happily remembered

as soon as it can be
fully forgotten.

all the goodness
of my life is
gone.

first you,
and with you
joy
love
freedom.

then
colors
trees
music.

even creativity,
which is always
the last to go,
is only making
a token appearance.

all my flowers
lovingly grew
I carefully gave to you.

how happy they made you!
how happy that made me.

when the flowers began
to wilt, i cried.

"don't worry" you said.
"i am growing a garden.
it will be ready
any day now."

the flowers died.

"nothing here to hold me"
you said and packed and left.

you had no garden.

I died tonight.
nothing here to hold me.

the layers I have put
around the pain of
your going are thin.

I walk softly through
life, adding thickness
each day.

a thought or a feeling
of you cracks the surface.

a call from you
shatters it all.

and I spend that night in death,

and spin the first
layer of life
with the sunrise.

all I need is
someone to
talk to
about
you
but
you
are the
only person
I can really
talk to. trapped.

I know our
time together
is no more.

then why do
words
come to mind
that call you
back?

Why do I plan
lifetimes
that include
you?

Why do I
torture
myself
with love
I never felt
while you were
here?

I was not ready for you,
but you seemed quite ready for me.

trapped in a week.
drained in a month.
deserted in forty days.

Forty days.   deserted.

Jesus spent forty days
in a desert once.
He was tempted by
the devil.
We are told he resisted temptation.

fortunately
for The Pope
The Archbishop of Cantebury
and Billy Graham
you were not the devil.

Christianity might never have
gotten off the ground.

What do I do
now that you're gone?

well, when there's
nothing else going on,
which is quite often,
I sit in a corner and
I cry
until I am
too numbed
to feel.

paralized motionless
for a while. nothing
moving
inside or out.

then I think
how much I miss you.

then I feel
fear
pain
loneliness
desolation.

then
I cry
until I am
too numbed
to feel

interesting pastime.

try it next time
someone cuts out your
heart
and hangs it on their
charm bracelet.

I write only
until I cry
which is why
so few poems
this month
have been
finished.

It's just
that

as the memory of your
light fades
my days grow dark.

my nights are lit with
electric bulbs. I cannot
sleep. I am afraid of the
dark. I am afraid that you
will return and then fade
again. I am afraid that you
will never return. I am
afraid that my next thought
will be of you. I am afraid
that I will run out of poems
before I run out of pain.

I must give you up.
I must give you up.
I must give you up.
I must give you up.
I must give you up.
I must give you up.
I must give you up.
I must give you up.
I must give you up.
I must give you up.
I must give you up,
I must give you up.
I must give you up.
I must give you up.
I must give you up.
I must give you up,
I must give you up.
I must survive,
I must give you up.
I must give you up.
I must give you up.
I must give you up.
I must give you up.
I must give you up.

i'm past the point of going
        quietly
        insane.

i'm getting quite noisy about it.

the neighbors must think I'm mad.

the neighbors,
for once,
think right.

it is cruel to
leave leaving
behind an intention
to return
        "soon"

and to send a second hand
"hello" three weeks later
with your new love's mother.

very cruel.

very you.

I have to get out of this.

I have to remember a time
when I was happy.

that'll take some doing.

Ah, I remember a time!

it was with you.

ouch.

When there are
joys
I want you for
sharing.

When there are
sorrows
I want you for
comfort.

I guess I'm leaning
on your memory
a bit much.

I am Joy.
I am everything.
I can do all things but two:

1. forget that I love you.

2. forget that you no longer love me.

although my
nature is not to
live by day

I can not
tolerate another
night like this.

so.

I will wake up
early
tomorrow, and on
very little sleep
do do do
all day long.

and fall asleep
exhausted tomorrow
early evening,
too tired
even for
nightmares.

This is it,
this poem,
the graveyard of love

where I will bury
    us
once and for all.

to give you up.

God!
what a bell of freedom
that rings within me
and I salivate.

no more waiting for
letters
phone calls
post cards
that never come.

no more waiting for
"The Re-Creation Of We."

no more waiting for your
warm body between
clean pressed sheets.

no more disected schemes,
or nocturnal day dreams.

no more creative energy
wasted
in letters never mailed.

and, after a while,

no more insomnia.
no more insanity.

some more happiness.
some more life.

all it took was giving you up.

and that took quite a bit.

My friends are still there!

neglected,
rejected
while I gave all my
precious moments to
you.

they're still here!

god bless them.

god damn you.

help me up
my friend.

dust me off.

feed me warmth

you are comfort.

let me lean on you
until I can stand
           alone.

I will then stand
a little taller,

and you will be
proud
to have a friend
such as I.

sifting through the
ashes of our relationship

I find many things
to be grateful for.

I can say "thank you" for
warm mornings,
cold protein drinks,
and all the love you have ever offered another

I can say "thank you"
for being there
willing to be shared.

I can say "thank you" for
the countless peoms you were
the inspiration for and the
many changes you were
catylist to.

but how, in my grasp of
the English Language,
faltering as it is,
can I ever

thank you
        for
Beethoven
        ?

the last day of my
loving you is
at hand.

in hand,
a pen, writing one of
the last poems
exclusively yours.

my pain fades,
as my love does,
as autumn did.

winter is too intense
a season to miss
someone in.

the last leaf
fell today.

the first snow
falls tonight.

THE SURVIVAL HANDBOOK

for Casey/Kathleen

The enclosed suggestions are simply things that have worked for me. They are not presented as universal truths, and should not be taken that way. You may have to adapt or discard each individual point to fit yourself.

One

You are not alone, first of all. Know this. As you read this, as you feel loneliness, pain, fear, depression, know that millions of others are feeling what you feel, for the same reason: A significant other has left their life.

When I first loved, and first lost, and first wrote poetry about it, I thought that I was the only one in the universe feeling that desolate. When the poems from this period in time were published I began receiving letters from people saying "Hey. Wow. I thought I was feeling these things alone. You seem to be feeling these things too." I was suddenly no longer alone in my loneliness.

Somehow the Camaraderie of similar suffering eases the pain.

You have comrades.

Two

Pain is for real. Whatever the cause, pain is for real. Feel your pain. Cry. Dive into it. You will not find it bottomless. In fact you may be surprised how shallow it really is.

Don't be afraid of your pain. It is a symptom of being hurt . . . it will not hurt you further. Only if the pain is covered, suppressed, ignored, intellectualized, will it surface in another, more hideous and uncontrollable form.

The pain will not last forever. The bulk of it will be over in ten days or less. Count the days. Feel the pain. It's not comfortable, but it's not all that intolerable. (Although it will be intolerable if you keep thinking "This is intolerable." Think "This is uncomfortable, but I'll survive", because you will.) Count the days. Ten or less. Really.

Three

If, in the back of your mind, you still harbor secret thoughts about your love's return; if you plan schemes and scheme plans for winning back your love; if you think you can bring a relationship back to life single-handed, the most important thing for you to do is to give up.

Recognize the simple, but brutally painful fact: The relationship is over. It will never be the same again. Never. Even if you and the other person got together again, it would be on another level.

Give up. Give up the dream. Give up the other person. Let the relationship die in your mind as it has in reality.

When recognized, you will find a great amount of freedom under the pain. A sense of relief. You have worked so long and hard, now it's time to rest.

Four

If you have been thwarted in love, you have been literally injured. You have been hurt. The phrase "a broken heart" is more substantial than random poetics. You have full right to suffer.

If you break a leg and are in the hospital, friends come bearing gifts, you get to watch TV with a remote control switch, you lay down all day, nurses bring you food and give you back-rubs. You are pampered.

If you have a broken relationship, you must show up for work and be as efficient as ever, your friends expect you to be your jolly old self, and you have to, in short, deal with a world that simply does not accept the fact that emotional pain <u>hurts</u>.

The solution to this problem is simple: Be good to yourself. Be very good to yourself. Pamper yourself. Buy yourself something nice. Eat out. Go to a movie, a play, a concert, a roller derby. GO!

Forgive yourself, over and over. Start by forgiving yourself for all the "mistakes" you made during the course of the Fatal Relationship. Forgive yourself as you would forgive your best friend. Extend that forgiveness to all areas of your life. Learn from errors, don't die from them.

Be gentle with yourself. Treat yourself with warmth and kindness. Don't be too harsh. For a while, in fact, don't be harsh at all.

All this boils down to: Love yourself. Care about you and what you do. Think how fortunate someone will be one day to receive all your unique and wonderous gifts. Consider fortunate you, who can, right now, give them to yourself.

Five

There is a point, and I think you'll be able to recognize it for yourself, where the healthy feeling of pain stops and a morbid dwelling in sadness begins.

The former state is real, often intense hurting. The latter is often laced heavily with self-pity, "poor little me," etc.

Leave the torch carrying to the olympic games and the United Foundation. You have better things to do with your life.

Starting will be slow, and the <u>real</u> pain will return many times. Feel it, and then let it pass. It will return less frequently and for shorter periods of time. One day you'll wake up and say "I haven't hurt in a week!"

It won't be long.

You'll survive.

Six

THE QUESTION OF SUICIDE

Keep it a question.
It's really not an answer.

Seven

It has gotten
to the point
where the
only
thing
that can
warm
me
is a hot bath

*Hot baths have magical qualities we mortals have
yet to embrace. No matter how bad you feel, a
half-hour after taking a hot bath, you'll feel a
lot better.*
Try it.
Right now.

Eight

If bits of self-pity begin creeping into your emotions, and you are unable to help yourself, then help someone else. Get lost in another's problems. Help them. Drive an old person to the store. Visit people in hospitals; people who have no one. Read to the blind. Talk to the lonely. Listen to the ignored.

You'll be surprised.

Nine

Some people are as adverse to nutrition as I used to be. Some of those some might read this book. I will therefore make four short health-type recommendations and highly recommend a book to those of you who want to know more about this most beneficial of subjects. The book is Let's Eat Right To Keep Fit, the author, Adell Davis. It has recently been published in a Signet paperback edition, and I have even seen it on sale in a supermarket, right in-between the potato chips and the chewing gum.

Nine-A

Protein is good stuff.
You are made up of protein, and look what good stuff you are. Protein does good things, and you should eat a lot of it.

The following things contain protein:

Vegetarians:
   yeast
   nuts
   soybeans
   wheat germ
   peas
   lintels
   beans

Semi-Vegeterians:
   milk
   cheese
   cottage cheese
   all other dairy products
   eggs

Pseudo-Vegeterians:
   Fish
   Lobster
   all sea food

Carnivores:
   All meats, especially liver

Nine-B

Some mouseachistic scientists threw rats in ice water and let them swim until they drowned. They then injected rats with B vitamins (not the same ones, obviously,) and threw them into the ice water. The B vitimized rats swam four times longer before drowning.

That those rats shall not have died in vain, let us draw a conclusion:

> *If you feel like a rat swimming in ice water,*
> *take B vitamins.*

Scientists and other rats aside, stress increases the need for B vitamins, and B vitamins, generously furnished, help the body fight stress.

I strongly recommend that you run, walk, crawl or swim to your nearest health food store and ask for Thompson's B-50 complex. (Any health food store worth its weight in toasted wheat germ should know what you're talking about, even if you don't.) Thompson's "50" is the most potent and least expensive B vitamin complex I have found. While at the store take two. On the way home take another. Every four hours thereafter take one. You should feel a difference right away (within the first two hours). Increase or decrease the amount you take depending on the stress of the day.

WARNING: Do not buy B vitamins at your local drug store. You might pay less per pill, but you get far less. Also, the dosage isn't balanced, and a balanced intake of all the B's is important.

Natural sources of B vitaimins are always preferable to pills. These include Yogurt, Wheat Germ, Yeast (don't buy it till you've tried it), and liver. Eating a lot of any or all of these will help a lot.

Nine-C

Vitamin C is cheap and very, very helpful. Buy a bottle of 500 milligram ascorbic acid and take three or four a day (one with every B vitamin capsule).

Nine-D

A good multiple supplement is good too. Since you're getting lots of B vitamins from the Thompson's B-50, I would recommend Plus Products Formula 175, Food Supplement without B Vitamins, also available from your local Health Food Emporium.

Ten

The human body is a wonderous mechanism. Strong yet delicate. Wise but gullible. Powerful and gentle.

The human body has the power to repair itself. Give it the materials it needs to heal (Vitamins, proteins, etc.) and beyond that, don't mess with it. What this means, in short, is keep away from all drugs your doctor does not insist upon you taking. If you expect to heal, heal rapidly, and heal properly, let your body do it. If you want to play human guinea pig with yourself, that's your right.

I know two people who were living together for about a year when they broke up. Both of them were, I would say, equally hurt by the separation. She went through hell for about two weeks, and was not quite herself for almost two months. He went directly to his doctor and threatened suicide if he was not given some drug to remove him from his pain. He was given stimulants and mood elevators and mood depressants and sleeping pills: a pandora's pillbox of goodies.

At first it seemed that the drug cure was the answer. He would be happy and seem relaxed, although slightly distant, while she was rarely seen, and when she was, she was in very low spirits. After a month things changed. She seemed to be getting along just fine, while he was more and more distant, glassy eyed, unproductive, and an all around drag.

To date he has attempted suicide three times, each time eating the entire contents of all his pill bottles. He is rushed to the hospital, his stomach pumped out, and released five days later with a fresh supply of pills. She has a new job, a new relationship and the only emotion she has left for her last lost love is pity.

This rather lengthy True Life Story only goes to illustrate the point: Drugs are NOT the answer. At least not for me, or for anyone I've ever talked to.

Also, when you get through all this, you'll be able to say "I did it Myself!"

Eleven

You have been through, and are going through now, one of the most universal of all experiences: Loving & Losing.

It is one of the most intense and emotionally overpowering human experiences.

Why not do something with it?

For example, did you know that you are a poet? You are. Honest. Prove it to yourself. Sit down with pencil and paper. (Pen and paper will do.) Find out what you're feeling, find a thought or group of words that fits that feeling, and write them down.

Now, instead of writing the words this way,
                            write
                            them
                            this way.

> *Put words that you want to*
> *stand*
> *out*
> *on separate lines.*
> *Forget*
> *every*
> *thing*
> *"they" taught you about*
> *poetry*
> *in*
> *school.*

Do this three or four times. Keep it up. You'll get a poem. Honest.

Rule 1: Line for line, poetry need not rhyme.
Rule 2: Honest clear expression of a fully felt experience is what poetry is
*   is all   about.*

Twelve

What creative things do you do? Want to do? Paint? Sew? Sing? Write? Bake cherry pies? Act? Whatever it is or they are: DO. You could well find this an intensely creative period. I always do.

Thirteen

Last, and Absolute-ly not least, on the list of things I highly recommend for survival is Transcendental Meditation.

The best way to survive the loss of a love is to grow out of it. Transcendental Meditation is the most profound, the simpliest and the swiftest technique of growth I have found.

In my other books I have devoted just a few words to meditation thinking that people are buying my poetry, not my method of evolution. However, this segment of this book deals with what I have found useful in the living that follows the dying of a relationship. I now feel at liberty, in fact duty-bound, to go into greater detail on the subject of Transcendental Meditation as taught by Maharishi Mahesh Yogi.

First of all, let's look at what Transcendental Meditation (TM) is not.

TM is not a religion. TM does not interfere with your practice or lack of practice of any religion. The Pope can meditate. Madelyn Murray can meditate. TM is not a discipline. It is not a form of concentration. It is not a set of rules that, if you live by them, you will be enlightened in ten or twenty lifetimes.

Now, what TM is.

Transcendental Meditation is simple. It takes thirty seconds to learn. TM is automatic. TM does itself through you. You simply begin the practice, and TM takes it from there. Being automatic, TM is effortless. You just sit back and enjoy. TM is a technique for reaching the subtlest aspects of your mind. Just as laying down and closing your eyes is the technique for sleep, sitting comfortably and beginning TM is the technique for reaching subtle aspects.

What the practice of TM entails.

There are no "don't" associated with the practice of Transcendental Meditation. No "don't eat meat." No "don't have sex." No don'ts. There is just one "do". DO MEDITATE. TM is practiced twice a day, when you first get up, and just before your evening meal, for about twenty minutes each sitting. Other than these two times, meditation is forgotten about. "Meditate and do what you want." is the slogan of TM. Giving absolute laws for relative situations is not practical. TM increases your ability to choose the most positive action in any given situation, and, after a few years, your actions are automatically pro-life.

What TM does.

Ah, this is the best part. By simply, twice daily, practicing TM, the following wonderous results come automatically. Increased joy, happiness, creativity, intelligence . . . all the things you look upon as wonderful will grow to their maximum human limits within you. Your interpersonal relationships will take on new meaning, depth and variety: being a more wonderous person, wonderful people will be drawn to you. You will, as mentioned above, be able to do the most pro-life action in any situation, and do it automatically. This supports nature in her one great goal: Evolution. Nature in turn will support you by fulfilling your desires, almost instantly. In short, TM brings man to his natural state of life, in the true sense of the word. No mystical assistance, no spiritual guidance, just man, fully evolved, at peace within himself and with the universe.

And how long does all this joy-joy stuff take? The state described above is reached with TM in four to six years. This means, for most people reading this, that the majority of their life will be spent as a fully evolved, loving-loved being; if, of course, they begin meditation.

There are many areas I did not cover: health, society, family, etc. Take my word for it, meditation has a projound positive effect on all of them.

The process of learning meditation is simple. First, an introductory lecture, in which the basics of meditation are given. Second, a second lecture where further details are given. Third, the teaching of the meditation technique. This teaching is done individually and privately with an instructor personally trained by Maharishi Mahesh Yogi. The teaching takes about fifteen minutes. This is followed by three meetings, about an hour each, on three consecutive days following the teaching. At these meetings the meditation is checked, experiences verified, and further comments about the benefits of TM are made. That's all — You are then a Meditator.

For further information on TM, and for the address of a local SIMS (Student's International Meditation Society) or IMS (International Meditation Society) center, please contact

SIMS
1015 Gayley Avenue
Los Angeles, California
90024

and, Jai Guru Dev

SIMS-IMS

STUDENTS' INTERNATIONAL MEDITATION SOCIETY
INTERNATIONAL MEDITATION SOCIETY

Area Coordinating Centers

ATLANTA
1827 North Decatur Rd.
Atlanta, Georgia 30307
phone 404 373-8228

BERKELEY
2728 Channing Way
Berkeley, California 94704
phone 415 548-1144

CAMBRIDGE
27 Concord Avenue
Cambridge, Mass. 02138
phone 617 876-4581

CHICAGO
828 Davis Street
Evanston, Illinois 60201
phone 312 864-1986

COLUMBUS
1611 Summit
Columbus, Ohio 43201
phone 614 294-7467

DENVER
P.O. Box 6182
Denver, Colorado 80206
phone 303 893-3480

HOUSTON
5 Chelsea Place
Houston, Texas 77006
phone 713 526-2582

KANSAS CITY
P.O. Box 11445
Kansas City, Mo. 64112
phone 913 753-2067

LOS ANGELES
1015 Gayley Avenue
Los Angeles, Calif. 90024
phone 213 478-1569

MINNEAPOLIS
2323 N.E. Garfield
Minneapolis, Minn. 55418
phone 612 781-6946

NEW HAVEN
Box 1974 Yale Station
New Haven, Conn. 06520
phone 203 777-6250

NEW YORK
23 Cornelia Street
New York, N.Y. 10014
phone 212 691-1170

PHILADELPHIA
3905 Spruce Street
Philadelphia, Penn. 19104
phone 215 387-1733

SEATTLE
P.O. Box 253 — Univ. Sta.
Seattle, Washington 98105
phone 206 524-6464

WASHINGTON, D.C.
2127 Leroy Place
Washington, D.C. 20008
phone 202 387-5050

SIMS-IMS NATIONAL CENTER
1015 Gayley Avenue, Los Angeles, California 90024   Phone 213 477-4537

a non-profit educational organization

I loved,
which was purgatory.

I lost,
which was hell.

and I survived.
Heaven!